# Contents

*Written by*
**Benjamin Hulme-Cross**

*Illustrated by*
**Fabio Leone**

*Series editor* **Dee Reid**

**PEARSON**

# Before reading Where the Dead Walk

## Characters

The Captain

Carl

Miss Darcy

Driver

## New vocabulary

## Introduction

My name is Carl and I am a servant to a Captain who fought bravely in the wars. Now the wars are over and the Captain has to find work where he can. One day the Captain was hired as a guard to escort Miss Darcy to Mortlake Hall but when the Captain told the coach driver where they were to go, a look of fear spread across the coach driver's face.

# Where the Dead Walk

## Chapter One

The Captain and I had been hired as guards to escort a lady to Mortlake Hall. Her name was Miss Darcy. She was tall, thin and her skin was as pale as her silk dress. We had to hire a coach and horses to take us to the Hall. The Captain saw a driver grooming his horses and went to speak to him.

"We need to get to Mortlake Hall by tonight,"
said the Captain.

The driver turned round slowly.  There was a
look of fear in his eyes and he shook his head.

"Why would you want to go to Mortlake Hall?"
he asked.

"What do you care?" the Captain snapped.

"Sir, you must have heard the stories about the
road to Mortlake Hall..." the driver began.

"I don't believe any foolish stories," barked
the Captain. "If you want our money, take us
to the Hall."

"Please sir..." the driver begged.

But the Captain wasn't listening. "I will ride behind the coach and the boy will travel with Miss Darcy inside the coach. Now get a move on."

Miss Darcy and I got into the coach. We heard the crack of a whip and the coach started to move. Miss Darcy stared straight ahead and her pale grey eyes were misty. I was thinking about what the driver had said about the road to Mortlake Hall. *What stories could there be?*

The road went through a thick forest and it would be dark before we got to the Hall. Maybe that was what worried the driver. It was good to know the Captain was riding behind us with a rifle across his back.

# Chapter Two

We reached the edge of the forest as the sun was setting and the evening sky was turning blood red. The coach stopped and I got out and went over to the Captain and the driver.

"I refuse to go any further," the driver was saying.

"But we agreed!" the Captain shouted angrily.

"No further," said the driver shaking his head.

"What are you afraid of, you coward?" the Captain snapped.

"People who pass through that forest, they..." the driver began.

"They disappear!" said a gentle voice. It was the first time we had heard Miss Darcy speak all day.

"People who died of the plague hundreds of years ago are buried in the forest," said Miss Darcy as she stepped down from the coach. "It is said that their corpses walk again. They are looking for fresh blood."

"What a load of rubbish! Let's get a move on!"

shouted the Captain. He turned to get back on his

horse but the driver followed him.

"I'm not going any further!" the driver insisted.

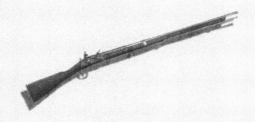

The Captain pointed his rifle at him. "You will

drive this coach to Mortlake Hall now or I will

shoot you!"

The driver climbed back on the coach and we travelled on in silence. We had only gone a short way into the forest when there was a loud crack and the coach tipped to one side. One of the wheels had broken. We would now have to face the terrors in the forest on foot.

The driver lit two torches and lifted two swords and an axe out of the coach. He handed the swords to Miss Darcy and me and kept the axe for himself. The Captain loaded his rifle and began giving orders. "Carl, you take a torch," he said to me, "and lead the way with the horses." Then he

turned to the driver and said, "You take the other torch and stay close to Miss Darcy. I'll guard at the back."

# Chapter Three

It was so dark I could see only a few metres of road in front. On one side was a long mound of earth. The torchlight made shadows flick and jump. What might be beyond the torchlight? The walking dead? I felt my heart thumping.

"Stop!" whispered the Captain looking back along the road. "Did anyone hear that?" he asked.

We all listened hard. Then we heard a strange creaking sound like rusty nails being pulled out of wood, or maybe like the sound of coffin lids being forced open. The noise grew louder and louder.

I looked again at the mound of earth. It was moving as if there were creatures inside. A sick feeling rose in me as I began to guess the awful truth. Then I saw an arm pushing up through the earth. I gave a piercing scream.

Hundreds of foul human corpses began to crawl out from the mound. The horses bolted and the Captain began shooting. The corpses were covered in mud but I could still see their rotten flesh. The smell of death filled my nostrils.

The first corpse headed straight for me. Its white eyes were gleaming through its muddy skin. I sank the sword in its chest. It fell to the ground and for a moment I thought I had killed it but then I watched in horror as the corpse began crawling back towards me.

# Chapter Four

More and more corpses kept climbing out from the earth and moving towards us. I heard a shot from the Captain's rifle and saw another corpse go down. Then he was shouting, "We cannot kill them. They are dead already. We have to run!"

"We can't outrun these creatures," the driver

said desperately.

But we ran anyway. Behind us the corpses

began to moan and howl. I turned to see

the driver climbing up into the branches

of a tree. The corpses soon caught

up with him. I watched as a corpse

closed its jaws onto his leg.

I heard him scream in pain.

Then I looked away.

As I turned, I came face to face with another corpse. I opened my mouth to scream again but the corpse reached out and covered my mouth. "We need a disguise! Cover yourself in mud like me," the corpse hissed. It was the Captain! I did as I was told. Then I realised that the driver was no longer screaming.

I looked around for Miss Darcy. And there she was, waving a torch around her head and calling out, "I have come so that your spirits may be at peace. Drink my blood so you can rest once more."

A small army of the dead crept towards her. She put her torch on the ground and stood quite still.

"Why isn't she running away?" I asked the Captain.

"I think she came here for a purpose," whispered the Captain. "She came to give the living dead the fresh blood they need."

A corpse stepped up to Miss Darcy and buried its teeth in her neck. She went limp and fell into the creature's arms. The corpses began to return to the grave, dragging Miss Darcy's body with them. As we lay shivering with terror, a pool of Miss Darcy's blood soaked into the forest floor.

# Quiz

## Text comprehension

### Literal comprehension
**p9** Why did the Captain point his rifle at the driver?
**p10** Why did they have to go into the forest on foot?
**p16** Why didn't the corpses die?

### Inferential comprehension
**p13** What was the 'awful truth'?
**p17** Why did the driver climb a tree?
**p18** Why did the driver stop screaming?

### Personal response
- Would you have obeyed the Captain if you were the coach driver?
- Do you think Miss Darcy is brave or mad?
- How do you think the Captain and Carl felt when they saw the corpses returning to the grave?

## Author's style

**p13** How does the author build up the tension before the appearance of the first arm?
**p17** What adverb is used to show how terrified the coach driver is?
**p19** Which metaphor does the author use to show how many corpses closed in on Miss Darcy?

## Characters

- **Driver**
- **Captain** (a fearless soldier)
- **Carl** (his boy servant)
- **Miss Darcy**

## Setting the scene

The Captain has hired a coach driver, coach and horses to escort Miss Darcy through the forest to Mortlake Hall. The driver warns him that terrible things happen to people who pass through that forest at night, but the Captain refuses to believe in any foolish stories.

**Driver:** I will not go any further.

**Captain:** But we agreed!

**Driver:** No further.

**Captain:** What are you afraid of, you coward?

**Driver:** People who pass through that forest. They…

**Carl:** They what?

**Miss Darcy:** They disappear.

**Captain:** You are fools if you believe that!

**Miss Darcy:** You might think we are fools Captain, but many years ago a plague swept through the villages. It killed hundreds of people.

**Driver:** They were buried out in this forest, well away from the survivors in the villages.

**Captain:** So what? There are plague victims buried in forests all over the country.

**Driver:** But people don't disappear in those forests.

**Carl:** But the plague was hundreds of years ago. Why do people disappear in the forest now?

**Miss Darcy:** For many years there was no explanation.

**Driver:** And people went on disappearing.

**Miss Darcy:** Then ten years ago, something happened.

**Carl:** What happened?

**Driver:** There was a survivor.

**Captain:**  A survivor of what? The dark?

**Miss Darcy:**  A man who people thought had disappeared came back. He made it back to the village we have just passed.

**Driver:**  I was in the inn when the poor man crashed through the door. I have never seen such terror in a man's eyes.

**Carl:**  What did he say had happened to him?

**Driver:**  For a long time he could not speak, he was so terrified. Then he told us what he had seen.

**Miss Darcy:**  He had been hunting near one of the graves just after sunset when something grabbed his leg.

**Driver:**  He looked down and saw a human arm sticking out of the ground and clutching his leg.

**Carl:** No!

**Driver:** He said the arm was old and rotten.

**Carl:** So what did he do?

**Driver:** He could not free his leg from the grip so he cut the rotten arm off with his axe.

**Captain:** So one man makes up a story about arms in the ground. Next thing you fools think there is a dead body in the forest making people disappear?

**Driver:** So how do you explain that the man died the next day?

**Carl:** Maybe he died of terror.

**Captain:** Then he was an even greater fool!

**Miss Darcy:** He was quite like you. He had been a soldier. Not a man who you would think was a coward.

**Carl:** I don't like the sound of what goes on in this forest at night.

**Captain:** So now you're a coward too!

**Carl:** No Sir, but maybe we should listen to them. What if there *are* dead bodies making people disappear?

**Driver:** As I said, I'm not going any further.

**Carl:** Maybe we should not go into the forest.

**Miss Darcy:** I do not wish you to argue because of me. I will go on alone.

**Captain:** Over my dead body!

**Driver:** *(whispering)* It might be!

**Carl:** Why don't we camp here tonight and travel on tomorrow?

**Miss Darcy:** No! It must be tonight.

**Carl:** I don't see why.

**Driver:** You could take three horses and I could take the other horse...

**Miss Darcy:** What about the coach? If you must go with me into the forest, then the boy and I should travel in the coach.

**Carl:** I think we should all stick together.

**Captain:** Enough of this, we are all going. And we are leaving NOW!

**Driver:** But sir...

**Captain:** You will drive this coach to Mortlake Hall now or I will shoot you!

# Quiz

## Text comprehension

**p24** What happened ten years before?
**p26** Why does the driver think the man died?
**p28** Why does the driver whisper the words "It might be!"?

## Vocabulary

**p23** Find a word meaning 'vanish'.
**p24** Find a word meaning 'reason'.
**p25** Find a word meaning 'grasping'.

# Before reading Dead Bodies

## Find out about

• what used to happen to dead bodies in the past.

## New vocabulary

**p31** dissect
**p32** executed
**p34** corpses

**p36** gruesome
**p38** evidence

## Introduction

Dissecting a dead human body is the way scientists discover how the human body works. But for a long time dissection was against the law in Britain. Then in 1752, the law was changed and medical students were allowed to dissect the bodies of criminals who had been executed. But soon there were not enough bodies of criminals for all medical students, so body snatchers dug up dead bodies and sold them to medical students.

# Dead Bodies

## Medical Research

Would you like to dissect a dead human body to see what is inside? That is what scientists do to discover how the human body works, but long ago in Britain, it was against the law to cut open a human body. Around the 1750s, scientists in Britain said they needed more information about how the human body works, so the law was changed and they were allowed to dissect ten bodies each year.

# Body Snatching

In 1752, a law called 'The Murder Act' allowed medical students to dissect the bodies of criminals who had been executed. But by the 1800s, there were only about fifty executions each year and more and more people were studying medicine. They needed more human bodies to dissect and they were prepared to pay for them.

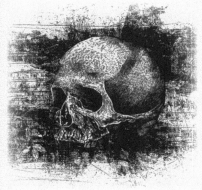

So some people began to sell bodies to medical students. These people were called 'body snatchers'. They would dig up dead bodies and sell them to the students. This was against the law but the body snatchers could get about £8 for each body which wa a lot of money in those days.

So where did the body snatchers get their bodies? They would dig up corpses out of graves a day or two after they had been buried. This happened so often that families began to pay guards to guard the grave of a loved one for a few days after they had been buried.

But often the body snatchers would pay the guards even more money to pretend they hadn't seen the body snatchers dig up the body!

Sometimes the body snatchers would dig a hole a short distance away and then dig a tunnel to the grave. Then nobody would see the grave had been dug up. They used wooden spades which made less noise and they always worked at night. They would take the bodies out of their coffins and take them to the medical schools.

# Murder

In the 1820s, body snatching became even more gruesome. Dr Robert Knox taught medicine at a medical school in Scotland. His students always had very fresh corpses. Knox bought many of these corpses from two men: William Burke and William Hare.

Dr Robert Knox

In fact, the corpses that Burke and Hare sold to Dr Knox had never been buried! Burke and Hare realised that an easy way to make lots of money was to murder people then sell the corpses to Dr Knox. That way they made sure they always had a corpse to sell!

## But how were Burke and Hare found out?

A lady called Mrs Gray was renting a room in a house owned by Hare. One day she wanted to get some clothes from her bedroom. Burke was there and he would not let Mrs Gray near the bed.

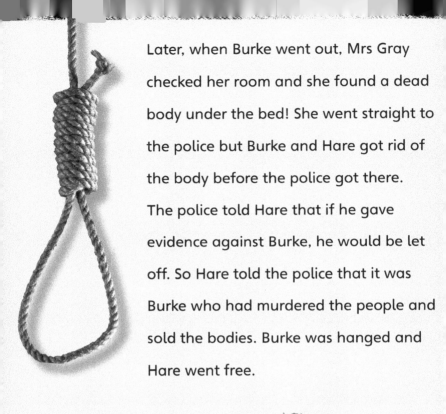

Later, when Burke went out, Mrs Gray checked her room and she found a dead body under the bed! She went straight to the police but Burke and Hare got rid of the body before the police got there. The police told Hare that if he gave evidence against Burke, he would be let off. So Hare told the police that it was Burke who had murdered the people and sold the bodies. Burke was hanged and Hare went free.

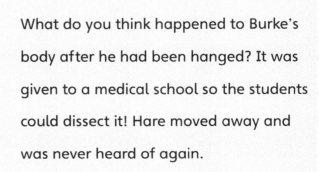

What do you think happened to Burke's body after he had been hanged? It was given to a medical school so the students could dissect it! Hare moved away and was never heard of again.

# Quiz

## Text comprehension

### Literal comprehension
p31 Why do scientists dissect human bodies?

p32 Why did body snatchers sell bodies to medical students?

p36 What did Burke and Hare do differently from other body snatchers?

### Inferential comprehension
p32 Why were executed criminals' bodies used for dissection by medical students?

p34 Why did the families only pay to have a grave guarded for a few days?

p34 How can you tell that the body snatchers were crafty?

### Personal response
- Would you watch a dissection or would you be too squeamish?
- Do you think Dr Knox knew that the corpses had never been buried?
- Would you leave your body for medical research?

## Non-fiction features

p31 What is the definition of 'dissect'?

p33 Point out three things in the picture that could be labelled.

p34 Think of a sub heading for this page.

Published by Pearson Education Limited, Edinburgh Gate, Harlow, Essex, CM20 2JE.

www.pearsonschoolsandfecolleges.co.uk

Text © Pearson Education Limited 2012

Edited by Ruth Emm
Designed by Tony Richardson and Siu Hang Wong
Original illustrations © Pearson Education Limited 2012
Illustrated by Fabio Leone
Cover design by Siu Hang Wong
Picture research by Melissa Allison
Cover illustration © Pearson Education Limited 2012

The right of Benjamin Hulme-Cross to be identified as author of this work has been asserted by him in
accordance with the Copyright, Designs and Patents Act 1988.

First published 2012

2023
16

British Library Cataloguing in Publication Data
A catalogue record for this book is available from the British Library

ISBN 978 0 435 07156 1

**Acknowledgements**
The author and publisher would like to thank the following individuals and organisations for permission
to reproduce photographs:

(Key: b-bottom; c-centre; l-left; r-right; t-top)

Alamy Images: Mary Evans Picture Library 33; Bridgeman Art Library Ltd: With kind permission of the
University of Edinburgh 37; Mary Evans Picture Library: Ronald Grant Archive 36; Shutterstock.com:
Anyka 32tr, 38tl, Bragin Alexey 31, dibrova 35, jumpingsack 1, 32bl, Lichtmeister 34, Lipowski Milan
31c, pra_zit 38b

Cover images: Back: Shutterstock.com: Lipowski Milan

All other images © Pearson Education

Every effort has been made to contact copyright holders of material reproduced in this book. Any
omissions will be rectified in subsequent printings if notice is given to the publishers.